THESE THREADS
BECOME
A
THINNER LIGHT

DAVID A GROULX

THEYTUS BOOKS

© 2015 David A Groulx
First Printing

Library and Archives Canada Cataloguing in Publication

Groulx, David A., 1969-, author
These threads become a thinner light / David A. Groulx.

Poems.

ISBN 978-1-926886-35-0 (paperback)

I. Title.

PS8563.R76T44 2015   C811'.54   C2015-907369-3

Printed in Canada

Book Design: Ann Doyon

THEYTUS BOOKS

www.theytus.com
In Canada: Theytus Books, Green Mountain Rd., Lot 45, RR#2, Site 50, Comp. 8
Penticton, BC, V2A 6J7, Tel: 250-493-7181
In the USA: Theytus Books, P.O. Box 2890, Oroville, Washington, 98844

 Patrimoine canadien   Canadian Heritage

 Canada Council for the Arts   Conseil des Arts du Canada

 BRITISH COLUMBIA ARTS COUNCIL
Supported by the Province of British Columbia

Theytus Books acknowledges the support of the following:

We acknowledge the financial support of the Government of Canada through the Canada Book Fund for our publishing activities.

We acknowledge the support of the Canada Council for the Arts, which last year invested $154 million to bring the arts to Canadians throughout the country. Nous remercions le Conseil des arts du Canada de son soutien. L'an dernier, le Conseil a investi 154 millions de dollars pour mettre de l'art dans la vie des Canadiennes et des Canadiens de tout le pays.

We acknowledge the support of the Province of British Columbia through the British Columbia Arts Council

THESE THREADS
BECOME
A
THINNER LIGHT

DAVID A GROULX

Acknowledgements

Some of these poems have appeared in

Temporary Infinity (USA),

La Verity (Australia),

Breadcrumbs Scabs (USA),

Do Hookers Kiss? (England),

XXX NDN (Anthology),

Alien Sloth Sex, Yellow Medicine Review (USA),

Rampike, Poetry Salzburg Review (Austria),

The Single Hound (England),

Red Ochre (USA),

Recusant (England)

The Prairie Journal, The Red River Review (USA),

Blackmail Press (New Zealand),

New Linear Perspectives (Scotland),

The Bellow Literary Journal (USA),

Istanbul Literary Review (Turkey),

Crate Literary Journal (USA),

Blue Collar Review (USA),

Two Thirds North Anthology (Sweden)

Seek It: Writers Do Sleep (Anthology).

MY LOVE LEAVES ME

Maybe you were right
maybe I never gave a fuck about anyone
not even me
maybe that's where it all began
down there on the street
the one you ran away from

We could have gone to the suburbs
could go that far
could stay downtown
and watch the fall
and the johns roll up and down
maybe you're right leaving me here
waiting
leaving
me in the rain
with the criminals and the poor

They told me you died last night
with a railroad in your vein
and I will be there soon
your art will be worth something then

all we are is the dead and the dying, the virus,
with half the moon in her eye
you're turning tricks again, say you hate it
maybe you're right leaving me here
with all my broken pieces
and a bleeding half night eye

we're burning all the sun, we're mission after mission

and maybe you never gave a fuck either
and that's the best thing you could have done

GETTING PICKED UP

Do you have a light?

                              Yeah.

Come sit with us?

                              Sure.

Are you queer?

                              No

Is that your girlfriend?

                              No

Yours?

                              No

Kiss me then.

                              Oh

Kiss me again

                              Oh

MEETING AGAIN

I just came in
and everybody is already drunk
they stagger around on the dance floor
and laugh
the women are tangled around the men
the tables full of beer bottles

I'm sitting with a woman I barely know
barely want to know
she talks endlessly about her job
her money
where's your old man?
out of town
she says

another woman comes up to wish happy new year
the one I'm sitting with grabs her
get your hands off my fucking grass

the one standing smiles at me
I'm not cutting your grass
she says

I know her
I tell my friend I'm going to the bathroom
I see her sitting with her date
we sneak out of the bar together
catch a cab uptown

just like old times she says.

MEETING AT THREE A.M.

we are like strangers now
you and I
you're not even dressed after all this time
you sit there in sweat pants and sweatshirt
so unkempt
I'm so disappointed
I stand there waiting
looking at you
trying to recognize you
remember who you are

just a minute.

do you want a drink?
yeah

we are strangers

you sit

come sit beside me?
kiss me.
can I kiss you?
You say

I touch you
try to remember you
smell you

try to remember you
I kiss you
and
suddenly
I want to forget

WAKING UP

I woke up on your bed
with you next to my body
curled like a cat
pushing against my body

a pale lever falling
on my skin
pulling sleep from my eyes

purring
with your hair in my face

SHOVELING SNOW

You're still naked when the sun comes up
sleeping with your knees against your chest
I boil water
watch the snow fall
get dressed to go out
and shovel the driveway
again
it's a hell of a long driveway

my ration of sleep gone

shoveling snow
before you leave for work
the banks piled high along the sides
soon we won't see the neighbors
driveway

I dust the car off

crawl back in bed
my hands frozen against your skin

WRONG ADDRESS

Are there guns in the house?

                                                    No

Are there children in the house?

                                                    No

What happened?

                                        I don't know
                                        Who are you?

Police
What are you doing here?

                                            Live here

What happened to the door?

                                        I don't know

Are there guns in the house?

                                                    No

What happened to you?

                                        I don't know

Who called us?

                                        I don't know

Is there anybody else in the house?

                                                    No

Mind if we check?

                                                    No

Stop that dog barking or I'll shoot it.

Hey I think we got the wrong address!
Goodnight

Next door?

THIS LIE IS LIKE A RIVER

This lie is like a river that
drowns all I ever knew

We sing
We dance
We go home

Watch flowers die

Listen to the wind come alive

See
the night falling

HOSPITAL VISIT

This sleep is broken
with the sound of the rain
singing to the asphalt

the needles in your veins
left bruises

the electrodes in your chest
have left red marks

the kind of writing that
disappears from the body

it will lie submerged, incoherent
like the rain

I WATCH YOU SLEEP

I watch the little tv screen above where you lay
sleeping
the numbers change from 77 to 80

when your eyelids twitch the numbers move down
to 74

when your body moves the numbers go up
to 85

but mostly I watch you sleep

wait for you to open your eyes

I wonder about dying and all the
times we talked about it

I want you to be dancing
instead of dying

herewith
and the nurse across the hall

the one you hate most

PRESENTS

At this place where
my mother's mouth
was wet with beer
was wet with her mother's
sad inheritance
and her father's old wrinkled hands over her mouth

silencing his secrets

in the Harmonic Hotel
she is dancing
dancing with her mother's shoes
and the shackles her father gave her

and tonight when she comes home
she will give these to her children

RAINY DAY

Everyday we look for work
everyday we find none
there are one million of us

the prime minister thinks
we watch tv and drink
beer everyday

some of us do

the minister of welfare said
we should buy dented cans of tuna
and save our money for a rainy day

but when your're drowning
you can't feel the rain

maybe we buy dented cans of tuna

CARTS

I can still see them pushing
their carts down
the avenue
a few plastic bags of food
some beer
brown children walking behind

after the cart is empty
they'll push each other in it
back down the avenue
past the houses

the sun falling on
their footsteps

REEL INDIANS

I thought when I first went to
an Indian reservation I'd see
reel Indians, riding horses
killing buffalo

just like the Indians John Wayne used to shoot

all I saw
were some houses that
looked like sheds
and some kids
playing with a bicycle
there were no horses
no buffalo
no tepees
just some kids
playing on a bicycle

TRAPPING

When you first meet a woman
and she finds out you're a poet
the only thing she wants
is for you
to write a poem about her

except for you
you didn't want a poem
about your tits or your ass
your lips or your eyes

what you wanted
was blood

A DISTANCE

I lie here waiting for you
while the minutes turn to hours

hour into days
days into night
and these are the most
loneliest

each kilometer turns to
miles, miles into hundreds
these are the longest

each kiss, to stone

UP

Key
up
Jug
up
Gangs
up
Line
up
Covers
up
Razors
up
Kitchen
up
Meds
up
Trays
up

MORNING UP

I could hear the horses
beyond the wall
going past

past the prison wall

the sound of their hooves
fade
pouring into the land

away
from this
place

CHAINS UP!

We rustle in our bunks
the smell of weed
and contraband tobacco
stuck to the floor

Our sleep creeping away
from the screw
the chains
curl from our sleep

We wash our chains
We dress
We work
We eat

Chains Down!

We rest
our chains
rest

MADE ANGRY

The blood splatters on the concrete wall
across the bolted down tables
his head hits the floor

we stop
our cribbage game
we stare
for a moment

still
its not always a surprise

he bumped into the wrong
guy

at the wrong time

the beating continues
till the screws come in

fifteen two

I say

RULES

These are the rules

No whistling on the range
Never tell
what could happen
after lights out.

It's easier this way

Sleep is time you don't have to do
your own bit

Lose your good time

To keep your respect

Keep your tongue

Lift it when the guard wants it to jump

Keep it still
and take your time easy

It goes faster this way.

VISIT RULES

Kiss me
at the beginning

We can hold hands
for an hour

Whisper about
the future

Kiss me again
at the end

The guards will turn away

Let go of my hand
hold the whispers

for the ride home

IF I WAS

If I was warden of this place I'd paint the whole fucking
thing black
If I was warden of this place I'd have the
inmates strip searched every day
If I was warden of this place the hole would always be
full
If I was warden of this place the showers would be by
hose
If I was warden of this place the lights would always be
on
and the furnace off
If I was warden
If I was warden

If I was a screw in this place I'd twist every inmate until
he turned over
If I was a screw in this place I'd fuck everybody over
for a goodtime
If I was a screw in this place I'd burn all the books
There'd be no phones or tv
If I was a screw the hole would be colder
If I was a screw I'd be boss

If I was a prisoner in this place
I'd yell "Take me to the hole motherfuckers!"
If I was a prisoner in this place I'd sleep when I dream
of getting even
If I was a prisoner in this place the warden would hear
me when I walked by
If I was a prisoner in this place
The warden and the screws
would know my name
and not my number

THIS IS MY CANADA, SHELIA

In my Canada it's cold enough for the cops to freeze
Neil Stonechild to death

In my Canada there are still two thousand
shell casings in Gustafsen Lake

In my Canada
Poundmaker was broken and harrowed, his flesh to
feed the earth

In my Canada we broke Big Bear too
and followed him all the way to his granddaughter's
womb

there we built prisons for
the land
the animals
and the brown people

We slept beside the water
before Mahigan died

In my Canada
I'm afraid to go places
this new Babylon
and new Palestine
growing sick

In my Canada
I can hear my mother cry
like a strong wind

ADDICTED TO HELL

Now we live here in the rain
my severed hands still taste this letter

working in the fields
when the sun was long
and the night was always torn in two

the moon deaf, hung over us

chronic angels
restless
wait for the wind

or the sun to rise

THIS GARDEN IS DEAD

This garden is dead
I pulled up the beer caps
harvested the cigarette butts
figured out a way to keep the cat out

I blessed the vegetables
cursed the weeds
nothing survived
except one lonely sunflower
and then it was gone
chewed to death
by the sun
insects crawled
over its corpse
its roots turning to dust

FIVE TIMES THE SOUND

I can still hear those niggers being beaten
in the bush, Conrad

I saw it on CNN last night

out on the street
the night before

and the Stonechild boy
on CBC

I dig the dirt
though it is hot

it scorches the blackness
I heard it again

broken spade after broken spade

the sweat like rain
drowning my skin

I hew it every fuckin night

OUR HOUSE

Stillness haunts this house, now
the rent unpaid
the yard mostly
overgrown
the shed burned down two years ago
the flowers were trampled by the wind
a sparrow fell from its nest
and was eaten by a dog
there is no talking
no singing
only a bleeding into this earth

there is nothing now
except some leftover sunsets

SPEEDING

I remember this speed
this is for you, for you
about you
and me
the speed we went
I remember
going past it all
the houses we lived
the animals we had
the sun coming
down on the water
everything was moving
moving past

the apples I picked
but couldn't eat
buried in the land
and never getting to taste

the mountains
speeding
wandering into the
prairie into the
water going past

all the plain
I baled too
ripping my arms
tearing my muscles
and dripping
skin into the field
the horses ate that winter
grew fat and then grew skinny
and sped away
went past
where I am now

I remember the 40 pounder you
gave me because I was thirsty
shared it with you
and those speeding by
I remember when your
father died and mine died too, now past
we loved them and left them
buried near the head frames of the
uranium mines
be near them again

A long ride we had from the fire
that brought it all down

this house where we
starved and crawled
past
my flesh burnt

still scarred
I looked at it
disappearing
still there

WE MOVE LIKE COMETS

We move like comets
on this highway
past this life
like road kill

these dark spaces
lit for seconds
pass by like comets

we move on
into the darkness
like comets
our eyes shut
our feet down
move on, through
it all
like
a plume of light
following
the darkness

I HAVE KILLED ALBATROSSES

These nights are piled up against the wall
they have no mercy on me
but lie staring back at me

I am out numbered
they will not speak back to me

only stare

the sun comes up
yet these nights wear on

they pile up
like
corpses

they will not let me sleep

I have killed albatrosses

I have killed albatrosses
and I look back at them with
my one broken eye

CHANGING DIRECTION

Will you watch me
go now
with your crippled father
still tied around your
hands
our lives change direction
like the wind
and some of us spin
like hurricanes until
we blow out
will you watch me
now living like asphalt

PAYDAY

The police drive by

all night
the poor have money tonight
tonight we will be livin' large
cooking in the backyard
boiling in the summer heat

the police drive by

We'll be pouring drinks
and running to the store
for chicken
all night

the police drive by

tomorrow we'll be working at
whatever we do
nobody gives a shit

after the landlords
are paid off
our backs
the merchants
holding out their hands like bums

and our children
will drink milk

with empty pockets

NIGHT A WAY INTO THE MASS

I remember dancing with you
shooting pool
with your daughter
while my wife and your
husband watched
from the table
sipping beer
and rum
the heat
the wet
the cool on our breath

I AM A SONG

I am my mother's song
she sang while she buried
her sisters

I am my grandfather's song
he sang in the lumber shanties
all winter

I am my grandmother's song
she sang while giving birth
to my father

I am my father's song
he sang while the blood
roiled in his chest

I am these songs
and I heard them
with my first breath

DAYBREAK CONCERT

inhaling the morning
still sleeping from the night before
my horns buried in your pillows
my wings
broken over your body
still asleep at the scene
all your letters
like broken glass
before your painted
and carved tables
from my body
and kneeled at these kisses

MASS

Fuck me, fuck me, she sings
I answer her call
to prayer
to kneel at her sepulcher
and am filled with incantations
I inhale her scent
like incense
my tongue on her
labia like communion
the musk makes
me swell
I rise at her alter
and she takes my body like the host
her body is like wine
on my parched mouth
I become like a fountain
collapsing
on her crosses

WITH WHAT THE CAT DRAGGED IN

Our bodies brown and naked lying
across the bed
I can still taste the wine
on your lips
and the smell of your
blue jeans
the smoke in your hair

your drunken smile
lying there waiting
to be kissed

CHANGING THE BLUE

I feel the fire in my marrow
she squeezes my hips
with her hands, her legs wrapped
around my waist
her voice flickers like a candle

trying to break her pelvis
with my own

I exhale the night
and lay on her lips

as she turns into dawn
and perfect stillness

THIS WAY OF MAKING LOVE YOU HAVE

I remember
what you looked like
what you tasted like, lifting myself
over your bedposts
sucking every breath from my body
cold like ice in my drink
spilling it, like lies on the floor
with wine on your whisper
wine dripping from
your tongue
driving me
into your mattress
I swallow every drop
to collapse

cigarette smoke
pouring out
of your mouth
guiding me to you
I follow the ember
heavy like the night
and pile myself into the darkness

THANK YOU

She tells me about the children we'll never have
and leads me down to a slow
kind of death

leaning into the heaviest piece of the night

harvesting my breath
and tasting it

She holds me
waves crash into the breakwall

She takes pictures of me pissing on some trees

and giggles

laughing as we go back to the car

we are like adolescents

screwing in the backseat

and growing up on the ride home

I love this kind of death

HOURS OF DARKNESS

The night is lumped against me
like stone
it breathes on my flesh
I feel its tongue licking
my body
wet and heavy like lead

I coil into it like a dead man
I come alive

I FOLLOWED THE THUNDER

We made good medicine
you and me
we were making messiah
with our bodies
all night
we could have saved our
heathen souls
if we'd stayed together

ACROSS THE STYX

I wanted to go down to the river with you
watch it freeze
watch the moon
get buried by the dark night breathing
heavy on my body
while cabs cruise collecting their
fares crossing the river like Charron

I see Aphrodite and Venus
standing on street corners
waiting for the parishioners
to roll, to stop

Achilles and Paris just stepped
out of the West
and stagger to the river
with the three headed dog
me and you are in here
this dark corner
and we've got ten minutes before the cops make it to
Troy
and it only takes me five

to get to Olympus

the Centaurs are rampant tonight
shackled to the bars
we could see them almost every weekend
you and me will be down here every
full moon to watch it all be told

We move like legends through the neon night
move like the river
rolling past

THESE BROKEN PIECES

It's been so long since I tasted
you and the whiskey on your breath
and gave you lies to sleep with

I feel the morning on your flesh
my torn bones lay still
across your body
while I stretch my shadow
over your bed posts

ME AND THE TAIL MOON

I waited for you
while the moonlight was melting
into flesh

its tail wrapped
around the darkness

its mouth gaping wide

swallowing whole pieces
of me

REMEMBRANCE DAY

Today is remembrance day
and the war pigs are out
with their poppies
and pleas

I wasn't there
I can't remember

They drag these poor old mother
fuckers out of their beds
into the cold

lay their reefs
wear their poppies

fire their howitzers

and nobody really knows what the fuck for

except maybe the dead

THIS BELLY, THIS TIME

I am here alone
in the belly of the night
with cheap smokes
and insomnia
and wonder if you are still sleeping

I wanted to send you flowers
from my grandmother's reserve
where she dreamed of playing the fiddle
with her Algonquin fingers and French lean
I imagine it was beautiful
but it never was

I imagine you are sleeping
still and heavy
I can hear the wind blow through your bones
like a chime
I can hear you breath
like a rattle

OUTSIDE THE WEST ONE NIGHT

Snowfall
covering the blood
on the sidewalk
ambulance drives away
leaving me behind with these broken pieces of your
heart and scattered over the tables of beer bottles
and ashtray tongues
I am drunk on loneliness

The night is fat with the smell of smoke
and full of hand prints from the people inside

JIMDADOIKWE

I wait for you
like spring from this crucible
of winter

I see the bruise
on your neck
and kiss your breast
I can smell the booze on your breath
I don't care
I can smell the smoke in your hair
and taste the curses on your tongue
that never bothered me
I make another wound on
your body and devour it

WHAT WE SLEEP WITH

The night covers us now
we can hide from heaven

your head still wrapped
around your father's fists
and your body covered in
your mother's mouth

I taste the blood on the walls
of your prison
every time we kiss

ASHES

I see Nanabush
I say, What are you doin here? You're dead.
He says
I ain't dead, you are.

I taste the meat
and it tastes like ash
and I eat the scone
and it taste like ash
and I make love to you
and it feels like ash

NO ONE WILL NOTICE

The world will not care if we don't make it
home tonight if we don't make it at all

The world will not notice when we blow the last light
out and feel our way around

The water will run down your throat. No one will care
if we stay out tonight

No one will worry about us
No one will care if we dance

THE DEAD

I crawl into your room
tired from counting the dead
tonight especially, there were so many
so many I don't want to remember anymore

there were so many, Jesus
thought he could save them all
he couldn't

all I wanted was sleep
there was so little

while the darkness drifted in
and filled my mouth

and the living inhale
memories of the dead

MOISTURE

Let me make love to you
only with my mouth

my tongue wander
over your fields and fences
gather dew with my lips

my teeth pulling flesh
my breath like mist
falling on your body

I DRAGGED MYSELF INTO EVERY RAGGED MILE

I dragged myself into every ragged mile
dragged myself into the light

as the heavens move
the sun creeps into morning

still
under the sewn sleep

still hunting whatever is left

of you draped over daybreak

while you lay

FIELDS AT SLUMBER

The sound
the rhythm of this piece of
earth
inhales
at rest
it slows
numb
laconic

sunlight sprints
over this earth
and is gone again

this earth grows brittle
falling
into slumber

DOWN THE ALLEY

I see a car coming down the alley
it's a cruiser
I just bought the kid ahead of me a case of beer
and am carrying my own

the cops stop and get out
"Do you know why we stopped you?"

"Luck?"

The cops say their blitzing the neighborhood
like they do every welfare day

They run my name over the CPIC
and while waiting tell them I'm glad to see them
and I thank them for keeping the streets clean
of the likes of me

They warn me about the dangers of that alley
I thank them and think
fuck you

PROCESSIONAL

We are being stripped down
processed like meat
it's all politics
it's all about power

It is the sound of a cocky young white boy
tagging a guard
Are you fuck'n crazy?

It is the sound of
batons beating
young pink flesh

the boy doesn't scream
he'll barely remember
being dragged into another
bullpen next door and pounded unconscious

we waiting in our orange suits
this Machiavellian processional

the boy's shoulder is dislocated
and there are no marks
a dedication to history

waiting, we look at each other
we are many
we are helpless
look at each other
say nothing
our eyes are closed
and see
we are deaf
and hear nothing
and like this they will
remain

so we can do our bit
without being thumped

I don't want to be remembered here
nobody does
We hear the boy moan
they stop
and four guards come out
the gorilla washes his hands
he's a tough motherfucker
and takes much pleasure in
pummeling people

washes his hands

and we all go back about it
like fuck all happened

and the young white boy
crumpled in the corner
will barely remember what happened

will do his bit
the hard way

I WILL NOT CLOSE MY EYES

My wrist through
this wire
lonesome for your hand

the northern lights dancing
on my brown marrow

it rains in my veins

I cleave life out of these prisons
my eyes
obey the darkness
the limit

painted with the night

your tongue bleeding
on my tongue
your lips bleeding on my lips

and I shiver beneath them

MUSE DYING

And now the world is dead
I have watched it from beginning to end

The ink is drying now
I am greeting the beast

its black holes are unfathomable
for me
they remain black

pools where language dies
prayers drown
with dancers
and everything that is me

the beast asleep now
writing poems
on my skin

sinking
back into
the darkness of its eyes

AWAY THE SEASONS

remember sisters remember
      sisters
                       the distant forget

    changes

                       these ways
lean to write on your skin
                         store
                  it in your heart
    sorrow
                      stories

to struggle   were told
death   create

EVOLUTIONS

spinning
      twirling
           whirling
                swirling
                    twisting
                        coiling
dying

the earth dances with me
      killing
           slaughtering
              maiming
                butchering

destroying
creating

FARMS AND RESERVATIONS

I wanted to stay at a writers' retreat, but I couldn't

find a ride

I wanted to join the writers' union, but I didn't have

the membership fee

I wanted to send out my manuscript, but I couldn't afford

the postage

I wanted to print my poems, but I had no

ink

I wanted to read my poetry, but the people were

deaf

I wanted to send out my poems, but they got homesick, so

they stay here with me

and we tire of each other

THEY SLEEP IN OUR GRAVES

From corner
to corner
to corner

we said our prayers
to the deaf
the dead
and the dying

they dropped zyklon b
and hydrogen cyanide
into our

abyss

benzene
into our dissipating bodies

our hollowed out eyes staring

at the world

WHAT RISES IN THE PAST

Stumbling to the past
groping to the future

settler sons with screwdrivers

plunging into brown flesh
of frozen earth
touching her spine

from the rupture we pour
like blood

THE MAD AT THE SOUP KITCHEN

There were so many broken people coming in
from the cold

a macabre ballet by a breed
of conformists obedient to the misery

carve up their loneliness with each other
chew on the darkness and swallow
the sad aspirations
of what was undone

the mad came in too
not cold
not lonely
nothing but hungry

there
they were abandoned

MY WOMAN IS A MAGICIAN

She causes wine glasses
and ashtrays to levitate
across the room at me

one day she will make
me
invisible

then disappear

THIS RAPTURE

I will not be taken in this rapture
Heaven's hidden to me
they do not know us there
this earth is rising
on this tongue

This plague will not enter
because of what happened
to Jacques Buteux
because of what happened
to Marcel Lemay

this blood is red

city of god is drawn white

Pontiac will not be there
Jack Wilson will not be there
Poundmaker will not enter

Heaven will not know
these songs
these dances

George Drouillard may lead them
but will not enter
White Buffalo Woman will not be there

There I will know no one
I will not be heard there
not even as a whisper

THIS THAT SLIDES AWAY

They say you came to me from under the world

washed this body with sage

that only you, Raven woman could speak to the creator

speaking to creation now

woman of the deep snow

this that slides away

BROKEN MADONNA

Turning the light into whispers
you cannot raise the dead this way
broken Madonna
gathering voices to climb
the heights of hell

the rest of me is wounded
for now I have memorized death
broken Madonna

you've learned to keep your distance from me
pouring these curses over my body
covering me in chains
take this wounded kiss
from these broken lips
this weeping Galilee

broken Madonna wishing

flooding rivers
and building cradles for your bastard children

raising love letter moons
with these broken pieces of music
and your lover's carcass, cut to pieces
will not wash the blood from your hands

the land is sacred
these fists are lonely
and these wounds never heal

moving the graves of old lovers
and the most dark
broken Madonna

GAS SNIFFER

He drinks homebrew
wherever he can get it

and gave up sleeping forever

now he believes
with time all over his one hand

his hand is his past

that is the one he talks to the most

KNOW

The white man wants to know
                    wants to know

where Indians come from?

I tell him we came from blue duck eggs
he laughs

I tell him that Indians were cut from government paper
he laughs even harder

and then I tell him
Indians are a figment of the
white man's mind

he stops laughing

Indians are outside everything he can understand

A PUZZLE OF BROKEN PIECES

They had moose meat on the
mission last night

Last night in the West Hotel
politicians got drunk and went
in taxi cabs
and brand new pick-up trucks
with young native girls
picked-up for a few drinks

Last night another young native girl
drowned herself in the channel

a runaway who found a way out
last night.

WE ARE LIKE MOTHS

dancing in the porch light

while the night grows colder

and the sun still rising

we play our mischief

while our children sleep

and the moon is half a witness

our wings gnaw on the darkness

our eyes swallowing whole chunks

of light

until dawn steals the world

away from us

SWING-CRACK

The police are dancing
with their batons to
whatever tune comes to mind

swing-crack
there is my welfare worker
swing
How come you don't work?
Where did you drink all your money?
swing-crack
she sings

politicians on TV swing-crack
am I my brother's keeper?
am I am I am I am I swinging
cracking

the landlord is coming
swing-crack
the food bank running out of food
swing-crack

it's Thanksgiving and
nothing to shoot
except twenty-five partridges
swing-crack

can you hear the tune?
swing-crack
can you hear it now?

It goes swing-crack
swing-crack banker
swing-crack miser
misery swing-crack
swing crack

DAVID A GROULX

swinging
swinging
swinging
falling

THE DAY THE MINE CLOSED

When the mine shut down
the ore played out
My father came home
and ate baked beans and planted a garden

His friend Wilfred dropped dead
the day after the mine closed
his work was done
work then rest.

younger men left
their wives left them
marriages fell apart

children without fathers
men without jobs

they left for the giant mine in Yellowknife
Westray mine in New Brunswick
to Pickle Lake, Ontario
anywhere there was work
broken families
drifted across the country
drifted apart

this is the way things go

THROUGH THIS LITTLE WINDOW

I can see the skinned and the un-skinned
who are at war
I can watch the birds and the wind
who are also at war

there is light and darkness
who are also at war

death will teach life a lesson
and it will not refuse
collapse into its loving
arms and trace

sight
lead me away with a stare
at the beginning

howl this night

touches this body of darkness
covering tithes of scars

INDIAN VETERAN

This Indian is
raiding

riding into
town

drunk on HBC rum
stained by smallpox
cannot get
served in a tavern
served in Holland, France or Italy
severed

cannot get by on this
this addiction
to the past
this country suffers

brown skin scars
rancid

A BARD'S CONGREGATION FOR BACCHUS

Poet passed out at the table
are you done with WWII
have you spoken of Emiot
and Kaschnitz and Mandelstam
enough
the ashtray is overflowing

the tequila is spilled
onto a difficult beauty

have you had enough
beer, wine, tequila
and laughter

your tabernacle is full of empties
the sermon fading
from moonlit memory

your chalice tipped on its side
the dogs licking what's left
from the floor

your parishioners stagger home
Saint Peter, Saint Saul
and the great fall
and the sacred blue
poet
are you done now
sleeping on your tabernacle

sacrificing yourself

stretching out your voice
that angels might hear
that god might dare
to answer

ME-BY-NUMBERS

They came
and swept up
five children
like autumn leaves
the oldest ran away
to a city back east
to be with our parents again
the other four
were left behind
to raise themselves
there was nothing to eat
and the second oldest brother
was caught stealing peanut butter
for the youngest brother
and they were swept up
from a basement apartment
and taken one
by one to a white family
these Indian children
too many they said
to stay together

this good they did

the two youngest
would be easy to adopt to mold
their short memories erased
the second oldest brother was beaten
with a canoe paddle
for pissing the bed

this good they did

this Christian family
the oldest sister's face was slapped
and her mouth washed out with soap

these backwards children
for telling them to "fuck off"

this good they did

the youngest daughter was
to be adopted and
the youngest son, broken-off
from the oldest brother
and the second-oldest brother
and the oldest sister
and the youngest sister
these child savages

this good they did

TORN ALPHABETS
(AN ODE FOR MISS BROWN)

The second most hateful woman
I ever knew
taught an alphabet
is as important as P is for punch
to the stomach
and vowels are silent
always
the word hate is spelled with a whoosh

Her husband was a small
bald fellow with black-rimmed
glasses he looked like he too
knew these words plus more
beaten
her daughter was ugly and
looked like she was in need of attention

her son was tall, athletic and handsome
the sun rose
she fawned over him
in the house across the street
from school
after a second bout in grade one
for she hated me much
and felt more abuse was good for me
and required

I forgot about
her and the smile she had
when I won some colouring contest
and the local rag came to capture our
rage in ink and the things I did not understand, but
understood
how I could not raise my hand after she'd raised hers

questions I did not care for
answers I did not care for
eat your Eucharist
bless me-bless Miss Brown
and Elmer the safety elephant
because crossing the street
can be as dangerous as grade one

A RIVER FLOWING

A river
has knowledge
if you listen
you can hear it

what does it say?

BUTTERFLY KNOWLEDGE

A butterfly speaks to you
if you watch
it flutter

its wings are lips moving

its language
feeling the air

ONLY MEMORIES LIVE

Am I listening to you?
I am not listening to you
What am I listening to?
I don't know

my mind goes back
back
to my childhood

to our town
where there was a young native boy
my age
found swinging
from a tree

near the new subdivision
the town was building

the other boys
white boys
he had been playing with
confessed

they were playing
some game
children play

why this thing happened
I don't know
Nobody ever talked about it
some things you want to forget

I think of it now
because I don't know

MOVING A SOUND

I am in two places always
I hear two voices
I hear two stories
I see two people when I look in the mirror
I know two histories

For I am
two peoples
I walk two paths

IT BIG COUNTRY

this country does not exist
this country only lives on the 11 o'clock news
this country only lives in Peter Mansbridge's
big mouth

it big country

this is not the country north of Belleville
this country was stared down by big government
goons with big shoulders

it big country

a country where people ask stupid questions
where you from?
this country
where meaning dies in translation
dogs fight over corpses

left on bridges that led to the
outside world

a hundred days pass by like nothing
and long missing and murdered

it big country

where all the bodies are buried

where windigos cruise
invisible and pale

north and cypress
long wasted and hwy 16
all the way to the downtown

east side

this country buries all of its fetuses
behind the school

this country
sweats when the ghosts speak

I TELL YOU

Take this kiss from my lips
like Odysseus to Penelope
rest your villain heart
bring your fire-light
the thunder that moves away
from us

kiss me for this body
a river
through me
into you

PUT THE GUN TO YOUR MOUTH

Put the gun to your mouth
this is the only one who
could love you
missing and murdered
this love can protect
your body
this sadness is growing
into a nation
this sadness is becoming
anger
this wasted healing
a body
Canaan
becoming
I can taste the mud
in my mouth

CREATING CANNIBAL

Racism is hatred
I react in anger
and all we learn
is anger and hatred

Our blood remembers
the Other

this hatred
we make together
we labour for it

exhausted we give birth

to violence

and eat our
own
children

AN IDEA OF PROGRESS

In our lives
we are longing for
intimacy and meaning
instead we get
ipods and apps
gadgets and gitmos

our things
become
our lives
our lives become meaningless

NAMING THE WORLD

I can hear the old man
        calling Coyote

He comes to creation
chanting
his feet across four directions
from the spirit world
        he touches this earth

he names it back into being

chanting the universe

JACK WILSON WILL NOT TEACH ME TO DANCE

Jack Wilson will not teach me to dance
this circle dance
this ghost dance

I'm not ready
I'm not prepared
for this hunt

I listen to
the thunder coming
I breathe in
the musky air

Jack Wilson will not teach me to dance
with a closing of the hand
a falling down of the hand

the Whiteman is coming

* NOTE: JACK WILSON WAS THE NAME OF THE ABORIGINAL PROPHET

CLOISTERED AND DRIFTING

After chasing all the lonely places your body
could hide
after the sweats rolled down these hills
after following the rivers to your mouth
after moving across this skin and
under your breathe
this mist is swallowed

DO YOU REMEMBER THESE SCARS?

I am lonesome for the snow

Do you remember these scars on my body?

Do you remember the rain like nails pounding into
the earth?

said you needed me to hold sometimes
said it used to snow in November

you walked with the wind

blowing against you
with the moon's jaundiced eye on
your breasts

waited at the crossing
for the trains

we waited for the trains
boxcars of rage

dark woman

you are the earth
standing like a star

dripping all over the world

A WAY OUT

This thing that crawls
      under your skin

I can see it
you know it's there
you show it to me
      when you open your mouth

you tell me that it hurts
      it hates Indians

I can sing this infection
away from you
I can dance this disease away
I can exercise this

with medicine
      laughter

About the author

David Groulx is a powerhouse of
contemporary indigenous poetry
having garnered critical admiration for his
deft and forceful wordplay, taking readers
into blisteringly honest reflections of
survival and momentary redemptions of a
hidden indigenous world in the underbellies
of Canada's major metropolises and small
towns.

Raised in Elliot lake, Ontario he is proud
of his Anishnabe and French Canadian
roots. He has 10 books of poetry published
winning various awards, appearing in over
a 170 magazines in 15 countries with his
poetry translated and published into both
French and Ojibwa. He currently lives in
Ottawa, Ontario, Canada.